SPORTS CAR DESIGN
BY MAE RESPICIO

CAPSTONE PRESS
a capstone imprint

Published by Spark, an imprint of Capstone
1710 Roe Crest Drive, North Mankato, Minnesota 56003
capstonepub.com

Copyright © 2025 by Capstone. All rights reserved. No part of this publication may be reproduced in whole or in part, or stored in a retrieval system, or transmitted in any form or by any means, electronic, mechanical, photocopying, recording, or otherwise, without written permission of the publisher.

Library of Congress Cataloging-in-Publication Data
is available on the Library of Congress website.
ISBN: 9781669079026 (library binding)
ISBN: 9781669078975 (paperback)
ISBN: 9781669078982 (ebook PDF)

Summary: *Vroom!* What is that roaring sound? It's the powerful engine of a sports car. Car fans love the sleek curves, wide tires, and rumbling, turbocharged engines in popular sports cars. Learn about the features that make sports cars some of the world's most eye-catching vehicles.

Editor: Aaron Sautter; Designer: Elyse White; Media Researcher: Svetlana Zhurkin; Production Specialist: Tori Abraham

Image Credits:
Getty Images: Vittorio Zunino Celotto, 13; Shutterstock: Alberto Zamorano, 28, BoJack, 18, Brandon Woyshnis, 5, 17, Camerasandcoffee, 22, Carrie Fereday, 16, Christian Delbert, 9 (top), D-Visions, 8, Dan74, 23, dimcars, 20, Dvector, 4, Gabo_Arts, 26, Gustavo Fadel, 19, Ickeda, 14, Mau47, 29, Mike Mareen, 12, Mike_shots, cover (top left), oksana.perkins, 1, ParabolStudio, cover (bottom), Renovacio, 11, Roberto Lusso, 9 (bottom), socrates471, cover (top right), supergenijalac, 25, The Image Engine, 7, 10, Tofudevil, 6, VanderWolf Images, 15, WinWin artlab (design element), cover and throughout

Any additional websites and resources referenced in this book are not maintained, authorized, or sponsored by Capstone. All product and company names are trademarks™ or registered trademarks® of their respective holders.

Printed and bound in the USA. 5853

CONTENTS

Special Sports Cars 4

Awesome Engines 6

Dynamic Design 12

Built for Speed! 18

Fancy Features 24

    Glossary 30

    Read More 31

    Internet Sites 31

    Index 32

    About the Author 32

Words in **bold** are in the glossary.

SPECIAL SPORTS CARS

Roaring engines. Sleek body shapes. Tight steering. And lots of speed. Put it all together and what do you get? A fast sports car!

Porsche Cayman GT4

Sports cars aren't like regular cars. They have special **features** to help them stand out. Peek under the hood to learn what makes sports cars so amazing.

Porsche 911 GT3 RS

AWESOME ENGINES

Lamborghinis have the perfect logo. What is it? A raging bull. A bull is powerful—just like Lamborghini engines.

Lamborghini Aventador

These incredible cars have V8, V10, or V12 engines. The engines have 8, 10, or 12 **cylinders**. The cylinders are arranged in a V shape. They give the cars tons of power.

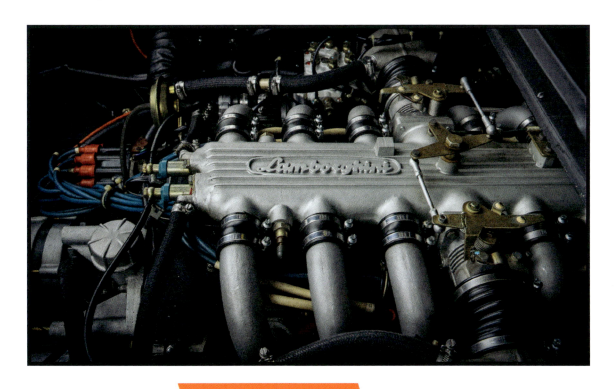

FACT

The Lamborghini factory has a robot named Robert. It moves each engine to different workers.

Ferrari factory in Maranello, Italy

Ferraris are made in Maranello, Italy. Each one is like a work of art. The engine is the heart of a Ferrari. Almost all of an engine is put together by hand.

Ferraris are famous for their V12 engines. The cylinders are perfectly balanced. They create little vibration to provide smooth power and speed.

Ferrari V12 engine

FACT

Ferrari's logo is a prancing horse. The horse is said to bring good luck.

Porsche engine in back of car

Some Porsche cars are different from other sports cars. Their engines are in the rear. Why? Rear engines shift a car's weight to the back. This helps improve **acceleration**, steering, and braking.

Many Porsche engines also have **turbochargers**. They give the engines an extra power boost.

Porsche 911 Turbo S

DYNAMIC DESIGN

Ferraris have sleek, **aerodynamic** bodies.

Their smooth lines help reduce **air resistance**.

This helps the cars go fast!

Ferrari Deborah

Ferraris being built at the factory

Some Ferrari body panels are made from **carbon fiber**. It is lightweight, but strong. It is the perfect material for these speedy sports cars.

Lamborghini Huracán Evo

Lamborghini bodies are made of carbon fiber, aluminum, and **titanium**. Every part is carefully crafted. Workers assemble the cars by hand.

Some Lamborghinis have side air scoops.

These special vents aren't just for looks.

They let air in to help cool the cars' engines.

FACT

The shape of the Lamborghini Aventador was inspired by insects!

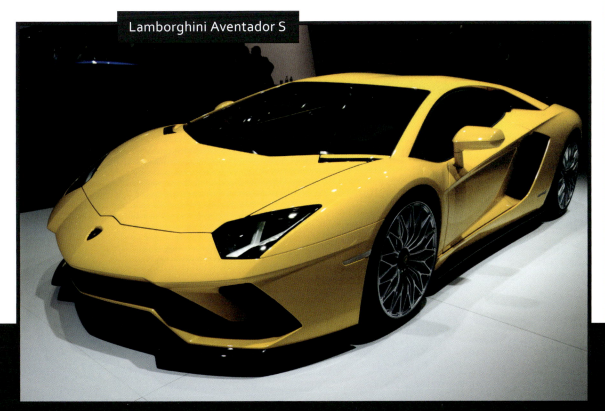

Lamborghini Aventador S

Rear wing on a Porsche 911 Speedster

Porsches also have streamlined bodies. Some have a big wing in the back. The wing isn't just for style. It helps keep the car stable as it goes down the road.

Porsche Cayman GT4

BUILT FOR SPEED!

What are sports cars best known for? Speed! Their lightweight and sleek bodies help them to be super fast.

Porsche Taycan Turbo S

Lamborghini Veneno

The fastest Lamborghini is the Veneno. It goes from 0 to 60 miles (97 kilometers) per hour in 2.8 seconds. Its top speed is 221 miles (355 km) per hour.

Porsche 918 Spyder

Porsches are speedy too. The Porsche 918 Spyder is the company's fastest road-legal model. It goes from 0 to 60 miles (97 km) in just 2.2 seconds. Its top speed is 214 miles (344 km) per hour. That's fast!

Ferraris are some of the fastest cars around. The SF90 Stradale goes from 0 to 60 miles (97 km) in just 2.5 seconds. Its top speed is 211 miles (340 km) per hour.

Ferrari SF90 Stradale

Ferrari FXX Evo

The Ferrari FXX Evo is even faster. It was built for racing. It speeds up to 249 miles (401 km) in less than 40 seconds. Wow!

FANCY FEATURES

Sports cars often have fancy features that set them apart. Some Porsches have **retractable** roofs. With the press of a button, the roof glides into the back of the car. Drivers often love zipping down the road with the wind in their hair.

Porsche 911 Carrera Cabriolet

Lamborghini Aventador with scissor doors

Many Ferraris and Lamborghinis have scissor doors. They don't open outward like regular car doors. They instead open upward like a bird's wings.

Scissor doors help the cars look cool. They also reduce the risk of hitting parked cars when someone gets in or out.

Luxury sports cars are very expensive. Few people can afford them. A brand new Porsche 911 can cost more than $100,000.

FACT

The Egoista is the most expensive Lamborghini ever built. It is valued at $117 million!

Ferrari Daytona SP3

Some sports cars cost millions of dollars. The Ferrari Daytona costs more than $2 million. The Lamborghini Sián Roadster sells for $3.8 million.

GLOSSARY

acceleration (ak-sel-uh-RAY-shuhn)—the increase in speed of a moving object

aerodynamic (air-oh-dye-NA-mik)—built to move easily through the air

air resistance (AIR ri-ZISS-tuhnss)—the force of air pushing against something; air resistance slows down moving objects

carbon fiber (KAHR-buhn FY-buhr)—a strong, lightweight material used for making objects such as car body parts

cylinder (SI-luhn-duhr)—a hollow part inside an engine in which fuel burns to create power

feature (FEE-chuhr)—an important part or quality of something

luxury (LUHG-zhuh-ree)—something that is not needed but adds great ease and comfort

retractable (rih-TRAK-tuh-buhl)—able to be pulled back or opened

titanium (ty-TAY-nee-uhm)—a very strong and lightweight metal

turbocharger (TUR-boh-chahr-juhr)—a system that uses exhaust gas to force air into an engine for more power

READ MORE

Adamson, Thomas K. *Lamborghini Huracán Evo.* Minneapolis: Bellwether Media, Inc., 2023.

Emminizer, Theresa. *Porsches.* Buffalo, NY: Enslow Publishing, 2023.

Flynn, Brendan. *Car Racing Records Smashed!* North Mankato, MN: Capstone, 2024.

INTERNET SITES

10 Fun Facts About Lamborghini
10-facts-about.com/lamborghini/id/62

HowStuffWorks: How Sports Cars Work
auto.howstuffworks.com/sports-cars.htm

Kiddle: Porsche 911 Facts for Kids
kids.kiddle.co/Porsche_911

INDEX

air resistance, 12
air scoops, 15
aluminum, 14

bodies, 4, 12, 13, 14, 16, 18

carbon fiber, 13, 14
cylinders, 7, 9

engines, 4, 6, 7, 8, 9, 10, 11, 15

Ferraris, 8, 9, 12, 13, 22, 23, 27, 29

Lamborghinis, 6, 7, 14, 15, 19, 27
logos, 6, 9

Porsches, 10, 11, 16, 21, 24, 28

retractable roofs, 24

scissor doors, 27

titanium, 14
turbochargers, 11

wings, 16

ABOUT THE AUTHOR

Mae Respicio is a nonfiction writer and middle grade author. Her novel, *The House That Lou Built*, won an Asian Pacific American Libraries Association Honor Award and was an NPR Best Book. Mae has fun childhood memories of cruising around California with her dad in his 1968 classic Ford Mustang.